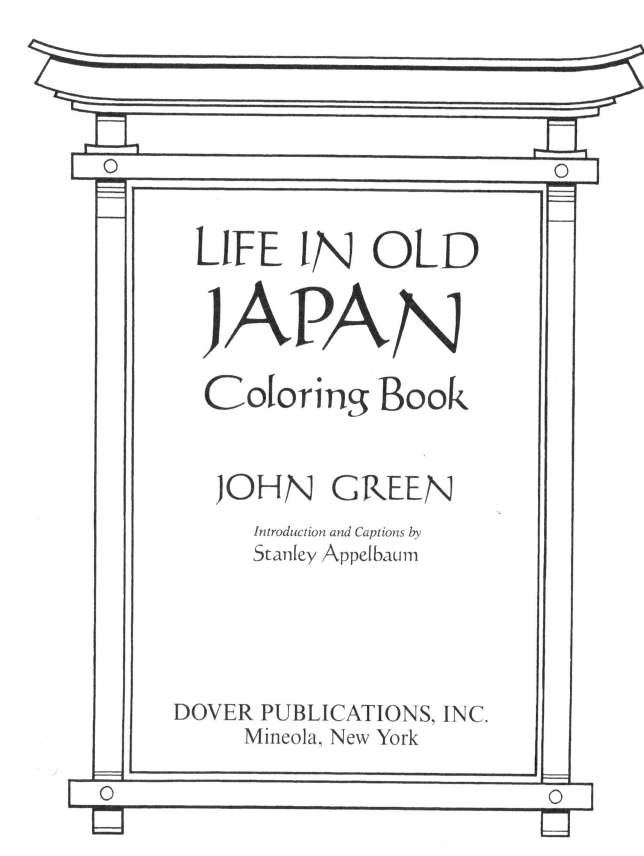

LIFE IN OLD JAPAN
Coloring Book

JOHN GREEN

Introduction and Captions by
Stanley Appelbaum

DOVER PUBLICATIONS, INC.
Mineola, New York

Bibliographical Note

Life in Old Japan Coloring Book is a new work, first published by
Dover Publications, Inc., in 1994 and reissued in 2008.

International Standard Book Number

ISBN-13: 978-0-486-46883-9
ISBN-10: 0-486-46883-6

Manufactured in the United States by LSC Communications
46883605   2018
www.doverpublications.com

Introduction

Japan has been populated for millennia and many striking art works are older than the time of Christ, but Japanese society and culture much as we know it became recognizable only a few centuries after Christ, when Chinese influence became widespread and Buddhism had been introduced. In the second half of the first millennium A.D., the authority of the emperors was usurped by powerful families of the courtier and military classes. Grim civil wars were followed in 1192 by the establishment of a military government, the shōgunate, the emperor remaining as a ritual figurehead. Further unrest culminated in prolonged civil wars in the 15th and 16th centuries. Toward the end of the latter century, the country was becoming exhausted as three strong generalissimos succeeded one another at the top of the power structure.

The ultimate victor, Tokugawa Ieyasu, established the shōgunate in his family in 1603, inaugurating the so-called Edo period of Japanese history, named for the shōgun's new capital in eastern Japan (the name Edo was changed to Tōkyō in 1868, the year after the Tokugawa shōgunate came to an end). It is this Edo period, 1603–1867, that is the subject of this book. A time of peace and prosperity after incessant warfare, it saw the blossoming of city life and mercantile pursuits as the watchful shōguns clamped down on the activities of the feudal lords. As the following pages will show, many of the features most closely associated with Japanese culture were either originated or else achieved their peak of development in the Edo period.

The book begins with the battle that made the Tokugawa era possible (page 4), then discusses the highest-ranking member of society: shōgun, emperor, feudal lords and samurai (pages 5–9). After a view of the country's main highway (pages 10 & 11), a brief review of the major religions (pages 12–14) is followed by the pastimes of the nobility and clergy: the tea ceremony and the Nō play (pages 15 & 16).

Rural pursuits will be found on pages 17–21, while pages 22 and 23 are devoted to the important occupations of shipping and mining.

Most of the remainder of the book is concerned with urban life. A street scene (pages 24 & 25) is followed by illustrations of: shops (pages 26 & 27); domestic life (pages 28–30); theater and other pastimes of townsfolk (pages 31–37); arts, literature, crafts and artisanry (pages 38–43); religious festivals (pages 44 & 45); and education (page 46).

Foreign influence and the final reopening of Japan after the years of the Tokugawa closure are the subject of the last two pages, 47 and 48.

Many of the pictures are based on authentic old Japanese woodblock prints and book illustrations, as well as reportorial illustrations by the first foreign visitors back in Japan in the mid-19th century.

Japanese names are given in the native order (family name preceding given name). Accents are used on Japanese names and words. All years are A.D. unless otherwise mentioned.

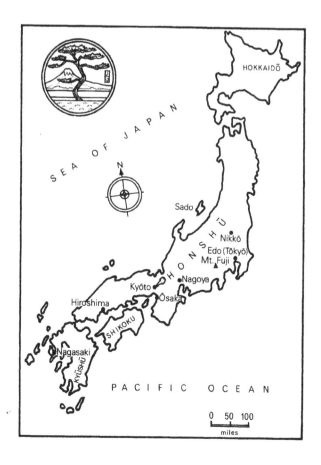

Tokugawa Ieyasu wins the battle of Sekigahara, 1600. This historic battle, fought in an area lying between Kyōto and Nagoya, all but ended the devastating civil wars that had long been waged between contending warlords for the mastery of Japan. Tokugawa still had to clean out pockets of resistance in the years that followed, but by 1603 he was ready to establish himself as the first shōgun (generalissimo, de facto ruler of the nation) of his family dynasty. The Tokugawas were to remain in power until 1867, and in these two-and-a-half centuries, although Japan was virtually sealed off from the outside world and in some respects was a totalitarian police state, it enjoyed a remarkable amount of peace and prosperity. Even earlier than 1600, Ieyasu had begun to develop the fishing village of Edo ("river gate"); now it became his administrative center and a rival to the emperor's capital, Kyōto.

Tokugawa Ieyasu as shōgun. Ieyasu (born in 1543) did much to consolidate the unity of the nation and the power of his own clan before his death in 1616. His extremely elaborate mausoleum is seen by every visitor to the popular temple site of Nikkō, north of Tōkyō. As with earlier shōgunates (the first was established by the Minamoto clan in 1192), the Tokugawa shōgunate was a hereditary military government, ruling by force. For most of the period 1603–1867, known as the Edo period, the shōgun was the most powerful man in Japan, at the apex of the feudal social structure. His successful control was made possible by the rigid class system already established in the country: (in descending order of rank) courtiers, military, farmers, artisans and craftsmen, merchants.

Katsura Imperial Villa, Kyōto. The nominal head of state, the emperor, had no power at this time (and, indeed, powerful ministers or shōguns had preempted the power of all but the most energetic emperors for many centuries earlier). The emperor, considered to be directly descended from the gods who had created the Japanese islands, was sacred, and much of his time was occupied by ritual activities meant to insure the welfare of the country. He and his court resided in relative seclusion in the western city of Kyōto, the capital since 794. The Katsura Imperial Villa, one of the most celebrated groups of buildings and gardens in Japan, was constructed during the first half of the 17th century on land granted by the second Tokugawa shōgun to the younger brother of the emperor, who had acted as an intermediary between the imperial and military courts.

A daimyō (nobleman) on the veranda of his mansion. The daimyōs ("great names"), or feudal lords, were the great landowners and masters of the samurai. The daimyōs usually had a castle town within their domain. Most of them had to spend every other year (for some, it was half of every year) in Edo under the direct surveillance of the shōgun. Thus, processions of daimyōs and their numerous attendants along the main roads of the nation to and from Edo were a frequent and impressive sight. Such travel was, of course, at the daimyōs' expense and entailed an intentional drain on their income. In the Edo period there were three kinds of daimyō: relatives of the shōgun; Tokugawa vassals raised to daimyō rank; and earlier daimyōs who had sworn allegiance to the Tokugawas.

Samurai practicing military arts on their daimyō's castle grounds. In one sense, all the members of the military caste, including the shōgun and daimyōs—all those privileged to wear two swords—could be called samurai. But the term is often restricted to the retainers of the daimyō, who held their land from him and might serve him in a wide range of capacities. Since the Edo period was one of peace, they no longer had much fighting to do.

The 47 faithful samurai avenge their master. Only occasionally in the Edo period was there an opportunity for samurai to display their loyalty and martial spirit. Possibly the most famous event of the era (1703) was the long-meditated vengeance taken by 47 rōnin on the courtier whose íntrigues had caused the death of their master. They thereupon took their own lives. They are buried at Sengaku-ji temple in Tōkyō. This stirring event was soon dramatized and has been the subject of puppet plays, of one of the most famous Kabuki plays (the *Chūshingura*) and of numerous films.

A way station on the Tōkaidō. There were several major highways, including five official ones, linking important cities in Japan. The most famous was the Tōkaidō (Eastern Sea Road), which hugged the Pacific coast between Kyōto and Edo. In all kinds of weather it was a scene of bustling activity. Daimyō processions (see page 7), merchants, messengers, chair bearers, priests, sharpsters and legitimate travelers crowded

the shops and inns of its 53 stations, made famous by the woodblock prints of Hiroshige toward the end of the Edo period. Even today the little towns of Akasaka and Goyu preserve many features from the past, and a Tōkaidō museum has been installed in a barrier gate-house at Hakone, near Mount Fuji (which is visible in the background of this illustration). Wheeled vehicles were prohibited to avoid the creation of ruts.

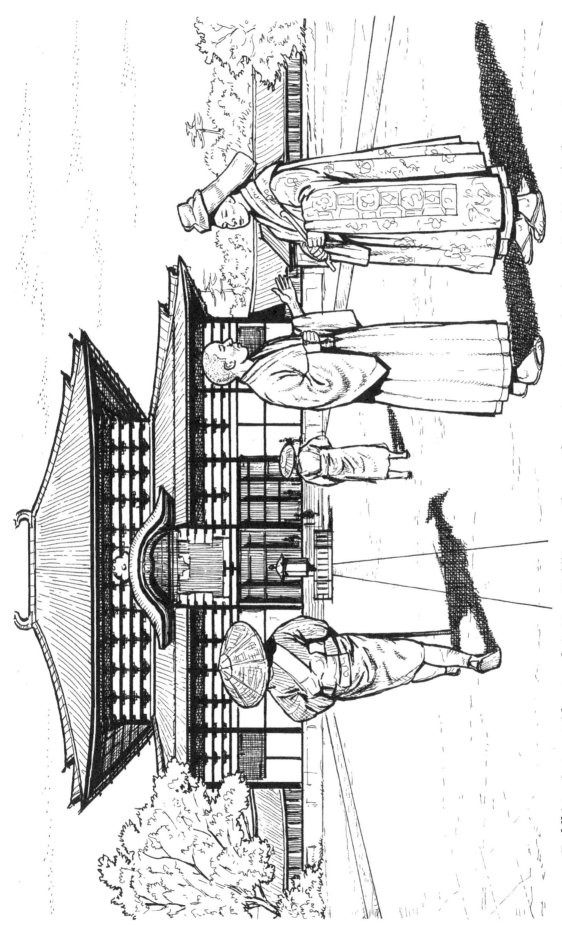

Buddhist priests outside a temple in Nara. Buddhism was the official religion of Japan in this era. Originating in India about 500 B.C. as a religious method for monks and nuns to attain freedom from endless reincarnations by renouncing the world, it developed into a broad-based religion of salvation for all mankind as it spread through Central Asia, China and Korea, reaching Japan by the 5th century A.D. In Japan it split into a multitude of opposing sects, some based on earlier Chinese developments, others entirely local. The sect most famous in the West is Zen, with its emphasis on meditation and sudden enlightenment. In the Edo period, every family had to be registered with a Buddhist temple. The city of Nara contains some of the oldest and most outstanding temples in Japan.

Shintō priest at the Itsukushima Shrine near Hiroshima. Shintō (the "way of the gods") is the truly native religion of Japan, with a rich mythology of nature deities and an animistic cult of sacred mountains, trees and animals. The emperor was believed to be directly descended from Shintō gods. The characteristic torii gate, one of the basic symbols of Japan, marks the entrance to a Shintō shrine. Shintō festivals and dances are particularly colorful. In everyday Japanese religious practice, elements of Shintōism are mingled with others from Buddhism and even other sources. In the Edo period, the shōguns kept careful control of all places of worship to avoid any opposition to the regime on the part of religious leaders.

Christian clergymen in Japan. In the mid-16th century, somewhat before the Edo period, Christianity was introduced by the Portuguese, who were then the most active explorers of eastern Asia. The new religion caught on quickly and there were an estimated 400,000 Japanese Christians by 1605. After some half-hearted government attempts to restrain this growth, Chris-

tianity was banned in 1614. The Shimabara Rebellion of 1637, in which poor peasants, many of them still Christian, revolted against their hard lot, led to a brutal repression and the almost total seclusion of Japan from the outside world for the remainder of the Edo period. Christianity, reinstated in 1872, is once again an important element in the Japanese religious picture.

A tea ceremony. Tea was introduced into Japan from China at a very early time, and some type of ceremony was connected with its enjoyment since at least the 8th century A.D. But all through the medieval period the ceremony developed in specifically Japanese ways until it was perfected very shortly before the Edo period. The ceremony was especially adapted to the life style of the Buddhist monks and of the warrior class. Nowadays, in its purest form, it is largely a rich man's hobby. A mind-purifying simplicity of procedures and of equipment is the keynote, but the necessity for a special hut in a special garden, and the practice of using rare heirloom equipment, make it a costly ritual—although, as with almost every human activity, economical substitutions can be made.

15

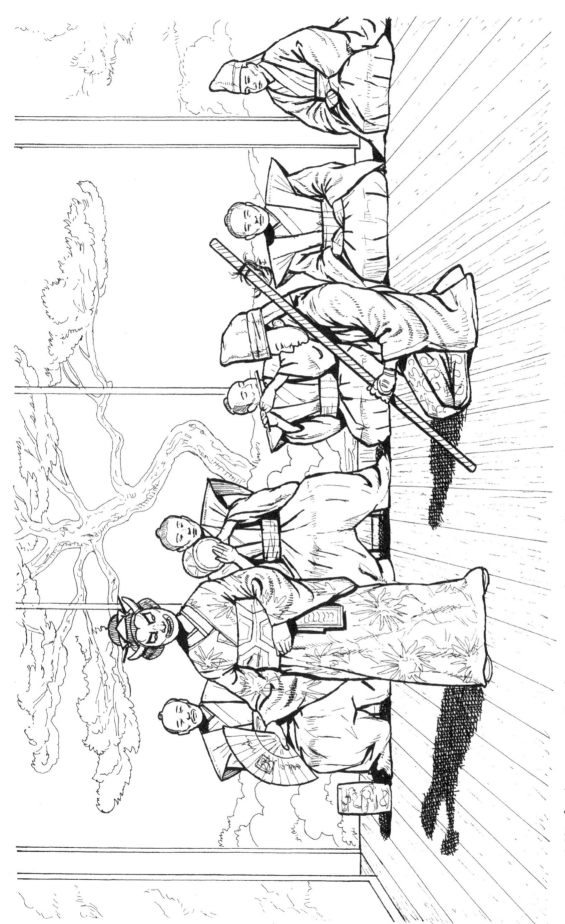

A Nō play in progress. Another amusement that is now democratic but was reserved for the elite through the Edo period, was the Nō play, the form of which was perfected around 1400 A.D. Performed on a special stage to the music of flutes, drums and chorus, Nō is a unique blend of drama, opera and dance. The costumes and masks worn by various types of characters can be great works of art in their own right. The subject matter is almost always tinged by the otherworldliness of Buddhism, although the main characters may be gods, warriors, demons or ordinary human beings. Nō plays are relatively brief, and several are usually presented at any given performance. They have been influential on European writers, particularly the Irish poet and dramatist William Butler Yeats.

Transplanting rice seedlings. As in every country before the 20th century, agriculture was the main pursuit of the bulk of the population in Edo-period Japan. And as in every country of South, Southeast and East Asia, rice was the staff of life. Land holdings in Japan were classified by the number of bushels of rice they could produce. Dry food crops were also grown, such as wheat and other grains, beans, sweet potatoes, oranges, grapes and other fruits. Also important were tea, cotton, tobacco, hemp and dye- and oil-producing plants. There were varied mechanical means of raising and distributing water. In the caste system, farmers came just below the military and above town-dwelling commoners.

Picking mulberry leaves for silkworms. One of the most important rural occupations was silk production; silk was a highly desirable textile reserved for the upper classes. The silkworms, actually moth larvae, were generally kept in special rooms in the farmhouses. They thrived on mulberry leaves, which were at their best by mid-May. After the worms had spun their cocoons, the threads were unreeled and spun into yarn. The whole process demanded a great deal of time, care and skill. In the background of this scene, another rustic pursuit is visible: renewing the thatch on a farmhouse roof.

Cloth manufacture in the countryside: preparing cotton for spinning; painting cloth. The women in the foreground, using a tool known as the kinuta, are pounding cotton threads preparatory to spinning. There was a wide variety of techniques involved in the manufacture of cotton fabrics. The men in the background are painting designs directly onto a length of material. Textile ornamentation was also done by tie-dyeing, with stencils and by printing, and of course there were embroidered textiles as well. Japanese clothing was simple in cut, but its decoration could be exceedingly elaborate.

Cloth manufacture in the countryside: weaving. Only a little silk weaving was done in rural areas; on the other hand, hemp and cotton weaving was widespread. Tasks that followed weaving might include dyeing, bleaching, shrinking, special shaping, stretching and flattening, and, of course, tailoring. Farmers were allowed only hemp, flax or cotton garments. Samurai were not allowed to wear satin.

Fishing with cormorants. Surrounded by seas, the Japanese have always made fish and seafood an important part of their diet. In the Edo period, merchants operated coastal fleets, and river and canal fish were also caught. Fish was eaten fresh—cooked or raw—or might be salted or dried for future consumption or for use as a flavoring. A special type of fishing—even

indulged in as a sport by the nobility—made use of cormorants. The birds were leashed and had tight rings on their necks to prevent them from swallowing the fish they caught. Cormorant fishing is still practiced in several places in Japan as a tourist attraction.

Shipyard. After the closing of Japan in the 1630s (see page 14), only a handful of foreigners could enter the country and Japanese could not travel or ship material outside, so that oceangoing vessels were no longer built; but coastal, river and interisland shipping was intense and shipbuilding was an important craft. As the Edo period progressed, shipping lines were ratio-nalized for more efficient rice delivery with less pil-ferage and spoilage. Extensive, projecting cabins (as on the ship in the background) were common on the coastal vessels, which had a single hemp sail and 30 or 40 rowers. Smuggling and illicit foreign trade were carried on in the far west, far from the watchful eyes of the shōgun.

Gold mining. A little panning was done for alluvial gold, but the sinking of shafts and tunneling was a more important method. Gold had been known on Sado Island (see map) even earlier, but new discoveries around the beginning of the Edo period led to the island's being placed under the direct supervision of the shōgunate. The overseers were samurai and working conditions were unpleasant. Japanese coinage was not uniform, but gold was the currency in Edo. Silver, copper, iron and brass were also used for coins, which were available in many shapes and weights. Paper money was used in a few outlying areas.

Street scene. The most distinctive feature of the Edo period was the growth of urban life. Even though artisans and merchants were theoretically at the bottom of society, in actuality they set the tone for the entire period. They had more ready money than the nobility, and *their* favorite pastimes, entertainments, art ob-

jects and customs were the ones that gave the era its special flavor. Shops of all kinds catered to their needs; there was a vast number of different urban trades and occupations, and a bustling entertainment industry. Streets were filled with porters, deliverymen, saunterers, sedan chairs, messengers and vendors.

A small street-front shop. The small shopkeeper, who might also be the manufacturer of his wares, was the most typical merchant of the era. The family lived behind the store. Sometimes shops of a given type were located close together, as in the street of dry-goods shops in Edo in the late 17th century, with street frontage ranging from 120 feet down to 9 feet. A German doctor who was allowed to visit Edo in 1691 was impressed by the rows of varied, well-stocked shops on both sides of the streets. They had displays of merchandise outdoors, and already at that time many of them were partially covered on the outside by a dark cloth—the typical noren, or shop curtain, still lovingly retained by conservative shopkeepers.

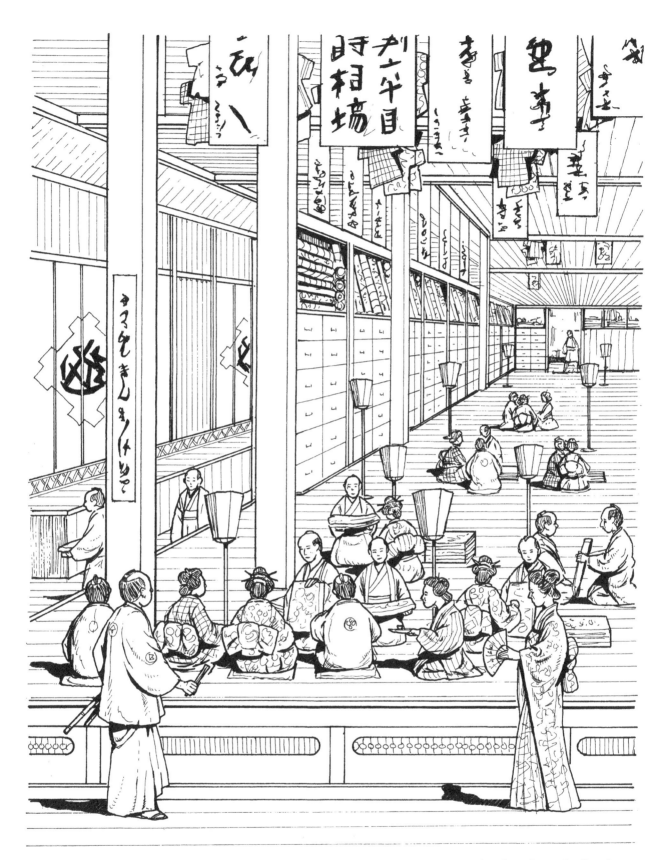

The Echigoya kimono store in Edo. There were also some very large stores in this period, such as the Mitsui family's drygoods store, the ancestor of today's popular Mitsukoshi Department Store in Tōkyō. Opened in 1673, it was innovative in its display of merchandise, and is said to have been the first Japanese store with female clerks. The family, from the small castle town of Matsusaka, near Nagoya, established important businesses in Kyōto and Ōsaka as well.

Townswomen at home making kimonos. In the warrior class, women enjoyed far lower status than men and were not educated outside their homes. In the country, women were not expected to assert authority openly. Even in town, women ate separately, but in general women of the artisan and merchant classes gained more freedom through the necessity of their participation in earning the family's livelihood. Waitresses, female shop clerks, servants and street vendors, musicians and entertainers were part of the daily scene. Household chores still claimed a great deal of women's time, cleanliness and neatness being essential national characteristics.

Townspeople playing games at home. There were many kinds of games and amusements for all ages. Board games included go and shōgi. Card games could even be quite intellectual when they involved recalling famous poems. Children's toys and games included not only the tops and cat's cradle illustrated above, but also types of tag, blindfold games, battledore and kite flying. The Doll Festival for girls and Children's Day are still celebrated today (on March 3 and May 5, respectively).

Townswomen making music at home. The lady at the left is holding a shamisen, often played with a plectrum. The stringed instrument on the floor is a koto. Other important instruments were the biwa (a type of lute) and various flutes, drums and gongs. Outside the house, there were professional street musicians; geishas who played, sang and danced for male guests in varied locales (see page 33); festival musicians; and the small orchestras and choruses attached to the different kinds of theaters (see page 16 for Nō-play musicians).

Sumo wrestling. This typically Japanese form of wrestling has very ancient religious origins. At first it was performed at Shintō shrines and Buddhist temples, admission money being used for the upkeep of the sacred buildings. In the Edo period, sumo became the sport, or National Skill, it still is today, although the matches still have a lot of ritual associated with them. In the contest, one opponent had to throw the other one down or push him out of the fighting area, which was demarcated by bales of straw. The auditorium included a drum tower that, in the illustration above, is just barely visible beyond the wrestler shown in rear view.

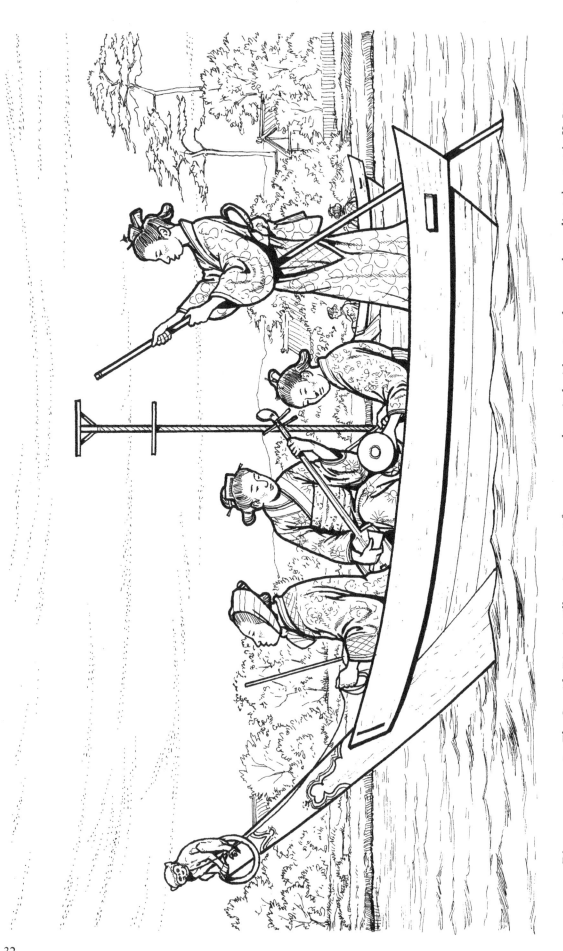

River amusements. The Sumida River is still an important factor in the life of Tōkyō today. In the Edo period, pleasure boating was a major pastime. In this view, based on a woodblock print of the 1750s, a monkey trainer and musicians are punting across the river to visit a shrine. River banks were also still associated in the popular mind with actors, because the earliest theaters in Kyōto had sprung up around the Kamo River at a time when acting was not yet a respectable profession. "River-bank folk" were those who could only afford to live outdoors or in temporary shelters alongside watercourses.

Riverside restaurant scene with entertainers. The Japanese have always been gregarious, and the townspeople of the Edo period were able to enjoy all sorts of public amenities that would have been unimaginable in earlier times for people of their rank. Eating and drinking places were plentiful. Various types of female entertainers could be hired for parties. Most famous and most expensive were the geisha ("artistic persons"), women trained from childhood in social graces and such accomplishments as music and conversation. The geisha of the Gion district of Kyōto are the most celebrated even today. In the Edo period geishas were among the favorite subjects of woodblock prints.

A Kabuki performance. The chief theatrical entertainment of town dwellers in the Edo period (and still popular today) was Kabuki, which originated in Kyōto early in the era. All the performers are men; those who play women's roles (onnagata) specialize in that area. Costumes and sets are elaborate. Masks are not used, but there are special wigs and face painting. Some of the action can take place on a runway (hanamichi)

that divides the audience area. The musicians and chorus perform offstage. Plots vary from historical and legendary to everyday urban events. The actor's art can include singing, dancing and acrobatics. Stage effects can be spectacular. Plays may be very long, and sometimes only selected acts are given. There are veritable family dynasties of celebrated actors.

Puppet-theater performance. The classical Japanese puppet theater, called Bunraku or Jōruri (also still performed), was the other main form of popular theater in the Edo period. It originated in Ōsaka. The puppets, elaborately dressed and ingeniously articulated, are quite large; just one of them can have up to three active (hand) operators onstage. The narration and dialogue are chanted at the side of the stage by one man, accompanied by shamisen (see page 30). The plots are often romantic stories of unfortunate lovers. Some of the finest Japanese plays were originally written for Bunraku and later adapted for other theatrical forms.

A street in the Edo theater district at night. The structures on the roofs on the right-hand side are theater signs. The buildings just visible on the left-hand side are tea shops to attract hungry and thirsty passersby. Street life is intense. Even though a bright moon is shining, people are carrying their own illumination. The illustration is based on a woodblock print by Hiroshige published in 1856, near the very end of the Edo period.

Basketmaker. Handcrafts and artisanry have always been exquisite in Japan, from folk products to the most sophisticated art works. Some of the craftsmen illustrated in paintings and prints of the Edo period include: gold-lacquer artist, raincoat maker, quiver maker, wooden-shoe maker, tea-ceremony ladle maker, rosary worker, binder of Buddhist religious scriptures, pillbox worker, paste maker, arrowhead-hole carver, saddle-flap maker, paper hair-cord maker and sword sharpener.

Cooper's shop. More of the unusual professions recorded from 17th-century Japan are: drum-cylinder maker, ear cleaner, inkstick maker, sword-guard artist, groove-cutter of handmills, mirror polisher, leather-socks maker, bamboo craftsman, mountain-priest's uniform maker, artificial-flower artist, plant-grafting master, seaweed-jelly vendor, rice-cake dealer, sweet-flag vendor, incense-pouch dealer and stick twirler (a street entertainer).

Woodblock-print craftsmen. Perhaps the best-known product of the Edo period in the Western world is the woodblock print, or ukiyo-e ("floating-world picture"). The townsmen of the day liked to see the subjects dearest to their hearts: actors in roles, beautiful women, famous places, wrestlers and entertainers, scenes of everyday life. Much of what we know about the period we have learned from such pictures (and a number of the illustrations in this book are based on them). The artist painted a design in black outline on thin paper. The blockcarver (background) affixed the design to a woodblock and followed the artist's lines, cutting through the paper. A different block was carved for each color wanted (unless a given color was derived from a combination of two others). The printer (foreground) pulled the prints from the blocks after pigments had been applied to them.

Store front of a woodblock-print publisher. The publishers of prints had their own sales outlets, and in Edo some small retail shops sold prints, too. This illustration is based on a book illustration of 1801 by the great artist Hokusai. The store front is that of the publisher Tsutaya. There were also traveling salesmen, street vendors and itinerant book lenders who dealt in prints. Great print artists, besides those already named in this book included Harunobu, Utamaro, Sharaku and Kuniyoshi.

Pottery and lacquerware. The Edo period was especially rich in "major" and "minor" arts. Korean potters brought to Japan as war prisoners developed the first Japanese porcelains early in the 17th century, and the various Japanese wares soon became world-famous, inspiring the earliest manufacture of porcelain in Europe. Lacquer was used for many everyday objects, like the oval box at the lower right. Ivory belt toggles (net-suke), decorative medicine boxes of different materials (inrō), textiles, painted screens, sword furnishings, calligraphy, dolls, flower arrangement and ornamental gardening are just a few of the art objects and visual arts particularly associated with this period of Japanese history.

The haiku poet Bashō on his travels. Some of the greatest Japanese writers lived and worked during this period, among them: Matsuo Bashō, the supreme master of the 17-syllable poetic form known as the haiku and author of the travel book *The Narrow Road to the Deep North*; Chikamatsu Monzaemon, the greatest Japanese playwright, whose scripts for the puppet theater were adapted for popular Kabuki plays as well; Ihara Saikaku, who wrote delightful novels about the problems and pleasures of the merchant class; Ueda Akinari, author of famous ghost stories; and Jippensha Ikku, whose classic novel *Shank's Mare* recounts the doings of a pair of adventurers on the Tōkaidō (see page 10).

A religious festival on a city street. Then as now, popular religion pervaded the life of city dwellers, springing to life especially in the many festivals (mat-suri) and processions that were felt as welcome diversions from everyday matters. Seasonal changes, local customs, celebrations in honor of various callings and

professions—all were excuses for pageantry, trials of strength and skill, spectacular rites, public entertainment and a carnival spirit of freedom from customary inhibitions.

Education. Among the warrior caste, girls were taught practical skills at home, and boys went to schools provided by the daimyōs, to learn Japanese and Chinese classics, calligraphy, Confucian ethics and etiquette. Schoolteaching in the towns was sometimes hit-or-miss; education was far from compulsory, and the teachers often had no formal training. In the country, many villages had a school that might be maintained cooperatively by the inhabitants; one 18th-century book illustration shows a classroom for boys and one for girls separated by a tall partition. Commoners probably received their best rudimentary education at temple schools (terakoya) in Buddhist temples and Shintō shrines.

Dutch traders at Dejima, Nagasaki. After the shō-guns closed Japan to foreigners (see page 14), the only Europeans allowed in the country until 1855 were Dutch traders, who had to live on Dejima, a small artificial island in Nagasaki harbor. Small as this community was, it was a source of Western knowledge for adventurous and forward-looking Japanese, par-ticularly in the fields of medicine, mathematics, navigation and military arts. (After 1720 it was legal for Japanese to read foreign books not directly dealing with the Christian religion.) The Dutch themselves reconstructed their European mode of existence to the limited extent possible.

Commodore Perry lands in Japan, 1853. The shōgunate became very weak in its last years, and when the vigorous, expansionist United States—in the person of Commodore Matthew C. Perry, who arrived in Japan with his well-armed "black ships" in 1853—requested to be allowed to trade with Japan, the reopening of the country was just a matter of time. The shōgunate collapsed in 1867 and in the following year the Meiji emperor was the first in centuries to become a true head of state. The feudal system was abolished, and sweeping social and political reforms made Japan a European-style nation without loss of its cultural heritage. Industrial expansion made it a world power by the beginning of the 20th century.